Negotiate with Confidence

Ed Brodow

American Media Publishing
4900 University Avenue
West Des Moines, IA 50266-6769
1-800-262-2557

Negotiate with Confidence

Ed Brodow
Copyright © 1996 Ed Brodow

This publication is designed to provide accurate and authoritative information in regard to the subject matter covered. It is sold with the understanding that neither the author nor the publisher is engaged in rendering legal, accounting, or other professional service. If legal advice or other expert assistance is required, the services of a competent professional should be sought.

Credits:

American Media Publishing:	Arthur Bauer
	Todd McDonald
	Esther Vanier
	Leigh Lewis
Managing Editor:	Karen Massetti Miller
Designer:	Gayle O'Brien
Cover Design:	Polly Beaver

Published by American Media, Inc.
4900 University Avenue
West Des Moines, IA 50266-6769

Library of Congress Catalog Card Number 95-83970
Brodow, Ed
Negotiate with Confidence

Printed in the United States of America
1997
ISBN #: 1-884926-50-9

Introduction

I love to negotiate. Do you? You better! Because like it or not, negotiating is one of your most frequently performed activities. Negotiating easily qualifies for the number one position among all the interpersonal skills you need, both in business and in your personal life.

Not a day goes by without some sort of negotiation taking place. You negotiate with yourself in order to get up in the morning . . . You negotiate with your spouse over where you will meet for dinner this evening after work . . . You negotiate with your boss for a raise . . . You negotiate with your colleagues over the timetable for a new project . . . You negotiate with the highway patrol officer who wants to give you a speeding ticket on the way to dinner. The truth is, you are negotiating constantly.

Ironically, we attend school for so many years and yet most of us never take a course in negotiation. They don't teach negotiation in high school. They don't teach it in college. Incredibly, most law and business schools don't teach it. So how do we learn negotiation skills? Trial and error.

If we're lucky, we develop some workable techniques for negotiating. If we're not so lucky, we stumble on for years making the same mistakes. Many people have a natural aptitude for negotiating. However, many people are terrified of negotiation and do whatever they can to avoid it. If you are one of these people, this book is for you.

◆ If you experience anxiety every time you negotiate, this book will give you the self-confidence that comes from a better understanding of what negotiation is all about.

◆ If you are one of the lucky ones who are "natural negotiators," this book will help you to understand the reasons underlying your behavior.

◆ And if you're not sure about how you might have handled a difficult negotiation, you may suddenly say, "Oh, this is what I should have done!"

About the Author

Based in Monterey, California, Ed Brodow is a keynote speaker, seminar leader, author, and consultant specializing in negotiation. Corporation and association executives from all over the world regularly attend his presentations on *Negotiating in the 21st Century*®. His clients have included AT&T, American Express Canada, Baker Hughes, Bechtel, Cessna Aircraft, Chrysler, Kodak, KPMG Peat Marwick, Lederle Labs, Microsoft, Mobil Oil, McDonald's, Revlon, Sun Microsystems, and Unum Insurance. Mr. Brodow is a former corporate executive with IBM, the Singer Company, and Litton Industries.

Chapter *One*

Why We Negotiate

Chapter Objectives

▶ Identify the attitudes that we all share when it comes to negotiation.

▶ Define negotiation.

▶ Determine what constitutes a good agreement.

▶ Recognize the importance of satisfaction in the negotiation process.

▶ Identify the two main types of negotiation.

▶ Identify the factors that motivate us in a negotiation.

A friend of mine called to ask my advice about a business deal. My friend is a professional speaker. It seems he deliberately understated his fee for an upcoming speaking engagement. The client accepted the lower fee immediately. After the fact, my friend suspected he had made an error. So he called me.

"Ed, did I do the right thing?" he asked.

"You know that your regular fee is reasonable, that you're worth it. What caused you to understate your fee?" I asked my friend.

"It was fear," he replied.

"Fear of what?" I continued. His answer: "I was afraid I would lose the deal!"

"Do you have any good reasons for suspecting that your client would have been unwilling to pay your full fee?" I persisted.

"No," he said. "I just wanted the deal very badly. When he said 'yes' right away, I knew I had asked for too little. I blew it!"

What do you think? Did my friend "blow it"? Isn't this a typical situation?

Many of us avoid putting our best foot forward because we have major fears about negotiating:

- ◆ I won't get what I want.

- ◆ I'll be taken advantage of.

- ◆ People won't approve if I'm too assertive.

- ◆ I don't like the feelings of anxiety I experience when I have to negotiate.

- ◆ I'm afraid of alienating my boss, customer, wife, husband, friend, etc.

- ◆ They'll say no.

My friend was afraid of being rejected. Rather than run the risk of rejection, he lowered his aspirations and relinquished his right to negotiate. He surrendered the most powerful social tool available to him because he was afraid of something that hadn't occurred, might never have occurred.

This story about my friend selling himself short is a good example of the attitudes on negotiation that abound in our culture. We have been conditioned to think and feel in a negative way about negotiation.

Many of us avoid putting our best foot forward because we have major fears about negotiating.

Recognizing Negotiation Attitudes We All Share

Here are some of the attitudes we share about negotiation:

1. *Negotiation* has acquired a negative connotation. Instead of regarding it as a useful and enjoyable social function—as they do in the Middle East, for example—we look at negotiating as something we occasionally have to do but would rather avoid. "It's slimy . . . It just isn't done" is the attitude of many North Americans.

    This book will show you how to enjoy the wonderful process of negotiation.

2. We believe that negotiation is a game that must result in winners and losers. The anxiety we experience over the possibility of loss ranks negotiation right after a visit to the dentist.

    This book will show you how to view negotiation as a collaboration in which everybody wins.

3. Largely due to our dislike of the process, we are in a hurry. We try to get the negotiation over with as quickly as we can. Negotiators from most other cultures are very patient compared to us.

    This book will encourage you to slow down.

4. Negotiation is thought of as the special province of experts, rather than a skill which is accessible to each of us.

    This book offers you access to a body of knowledge which is your birthright.

Each of these attitudes can be improved by learning more about the techniques of negotiation and by embracing the win-win approach wherever possible. Once you understand what is transpiring in a negotiation, you won't be afraid of it.

Developing a Definition of Negotiation

1

If you and I are in agreement on an issue, we don't need to negotiate. Negotiation becomes necessary only when there is disagreement. The wonderful Japanese film *Rashomon* recounts four characters' versions of the same event—each of them totally different. *As human beings, we are inclined to disagree!* You have your position on the issue at hand, and I have mine.

Agreement, however, is the prerequisite for living together. Civilization demands that we find a means of reaching agreement. Negotiation exists for that purpose.

Negotiation is the process whereby we overcome obstacles— our respective positions—in order to reach agreement. Negotiation is the most important social tool we have.

> *Negotiation* is the process whereby we overcome obstacles—our respective positions—in order to reach agreement.

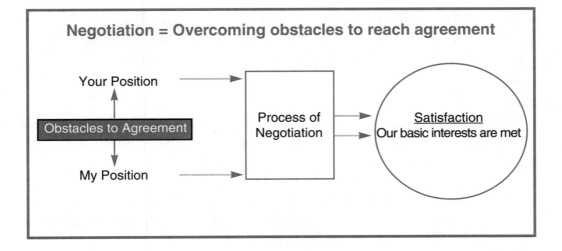

Negotiation = Overcoming obstacles to reach agreement

Your Position →

Obstacles to Agreement

My Position →

Process of Negotiation →

Satisfaction
Our basic interests are met

Negotiation is used to reach agreement on:

♦ Sales contracts.

♦ Goals and time frames for projects.

♦ Resolution of customer complaints.

♦ Employee satisfaction.

♦ Long-term objectives.

♦ Marital disputes.

♦ And many, many other situations involving differing viewpoints.

Of course, I'm assuming that both sides in a negotiation want to reach an agreement. Wait a minute. Did I just hear someone say, "Only if it's a good agreement"? That's an excellent point. What is a good agreement?

Satisfaction—The Key to Successful Negotiation

Satisfaction lies at the root of all successful negotiations.

An agreement can be regarded as good or bad, successful or unsuccessful. The key element that is necessary for an agreement to be successful is satisfaction:

♦ A *good deal* or agreement is one in which satisfaction is achieved.

♦ *Satisfaction* means that one's basic interests/needs have been fulfilled.

♦ We feel satisfied at the end of a negotiation if we believe that our basic interests have been fulfilled. Satisfaction lies at the root of all successful negotiations.

1

Two Main Types of Negotiation

In an *adversarial negotiation,* an agreement is successful if *your* basic interests are fulfilled. In a *cooperative negotiation,* an agreement is successful if the interests of *both sides* are fulfilled. Let's take a closer look at these two approaches to negotiation.

◆ **Adversarial (competitive) negotiation**
Negotiation is a contest. Each side attempts to realize its own interests—at the expense of the other side, if necessary. You win and I lose, or I win and you lose, or maybe we both lose. This is the kind of hard-nosed conflict that has become synonymous with negotiation. A good example is what goes on in most legal situations. There is a winner and there is a loser. Many of us dislike the negotiation process because we perceive negotiation as a contest. If you are afraid of losing, you will experience anxiety (as my friend did).

> In *adversarial negotiation,* each side attempts to realize its own interest.

◆ **Cooperative (win-win) negotiation**
Negotiation is a collaboration. Both sides work together to achieve mutual satisfaction. You win and I win. This is a newer concept that is beginning to achieve acceptance. In a win-win negotiation, the anxiety that normally accompanies the process is missing because we accept the premise that both of us can be winners. We perceive negotiation as a collaboration rather than as a contest.

> In *cooperative negotiation,* both sides work together to achieve mutual satisfaction.

This book will examine both types of negotiation. We live in a world where adversarial negotiating is the norm. We need to understand the dynamics of adversarial negotiating in order to survive. However, I believe that our future lies in cooperative negotiating. This book will offer a method for transforming an adversarial situation into a collaborative relationship.

Take a Moment

1. What makes you feel satisfied at the end of a negotiation?

   _____

2. Think back to your last negotiation. Was it adversarial or cooperative? Why?

   _____

What Motivates Us in a Negotiation?

I just defined *satisfaction* as the realization of our basic interests. However, we often confuse our basic interests with our position. At this point, let's clarify the difference between one's position and one's basic interests.

Positions have to do with what we say we *want* in the negotiation. *Basic interests* have to do with our *motivation*— what we really need to get from the negotiation.

For example, your position may be that you won't pay more than a certain amount when buying a car. "I won't pay more than the dealer's cost," you declare. However, your basic interest is to replace your broken-down old car so you can drive to work on Monday. Consequently, you wind up paying more than you said you would—and you feel okay.

Try to avoid being sidetracked by the other negotiator's position. Your focus should be on that person's basic interests. If you can discover the person's real needs and show him or her a way to fulfill those needs, you will be a successful negotiator.

What Do Our Basic Interests Look Like?

Our basic interests do not always involve tangible results. Material gain is only one of the reasons we negotiate. We are often compelled by drives that have nothing to do with the material outcome and which may not be obvious on the surface of the negotiation.

For example, you may be willing to pay more for an automobile at the local dealership because you don't have the time or inclination to travel to another city that has several dealerships where you might negotiate a better deal. Saving money isn't as important to you as saving time. Or you may be unwilling to raise your offer to the dealer because, even though you love the car, you don't like the dealer's snotty attitude. So you walk out. Your ego takes precedence over the more practical consideration—getting the car you want.

Positions have to do with what we say we want in the negotiation. *Basic interests* have to do with what we really need to get from the negotiation.

Primary Motivations in a Negotiation

Here are some examples of basic interests/needs—some of the reasons why we negotiate as we do:

1

- **Material gain:** Making a profit or obtaining a tangible benefit. We are motivated by the desire to gain something, or by the fear of loss.

- **Ego:** Pride and self-esteem. Each of us wants to be perceived and treated in a certain way. Madison Avenue understands that this is why people buy expensive automobiles. How we appear may be more important than material gain.

- **The need to win:** Some of us are very competitive. We just can't stand the idea of someone else doing better than us.

- **Control:** We like to feel that we have control over the situation and/or the people.

- **Fear—the need to trust:** We need to feel that we can depend on the other person.

- **Acceptance of others:** We want and need other people's approval.

- **Job pressure:** Do you need a certain outcome to protect your job?

- **Time:** Are you in a hurry? Do you have a deadline? Time is a major influence in many negotiations.

- **Desire for fairness/cooperation:** Sometimes we need to feel that the outcome of the negotiation is fair.

> **Our basic interests do not always involve tangible results. Material gain is only one of the reasons we negotiate.**

You must know what someone's basic interests are in order to give that person a sense of satisfaction. If you agree to a person's position, that person still may not be satisfied because you haven't addressed his or her real needs. On the other hand, you can give the person satisfaction without giving in to that position—if you address the motivation behind his or her position. We'll explore this further in Chapter 4.

Take a Moment

You're at the car dealership attempting to buy a new car. You're willing to pay $18,000, which is what your neighbor paid for the same car. (She was very proud that she paid less than the $20,000 sticker price.) The dealer tells you that he will not accept any less than the sticker price of $20,000. You tell him that you are prepared to pay only $16,000. The dealer has had a very slow month. He is one car short of making his incentive bonus. In other words, if he sells one more car, he will receive a huge incentive payment from the manufacturer. Answers appear on page 94.

1. What is your position?

    _____

2. What is your real interest?

    _____

3. What is the dealer's position?

    _____

4. What is the dealer's real interest?

    _____

5. How can the interests of both sides be accommodated?

    _____

Having completed this exercise, you now have a better understanding of the difference between positions and basic interests—between what people say they want as opposed to what they really need to get from a negotiation. This exercise demonstrates how much easier it is to reach an agreement when you understand the underlying motivation of the parties.

Negotiation is a game in which everybody can be a winner. Your anxiety will disappear when you recognize that both sides can have their needs met. This book will show you how to enjoy the process of negotiation. In Chapter 2, we will take a look at the characteristics of successful negotiators.

Self-Check: Chapter 1 Review

Answers to the following questions appear on page 94.

1

1. Negotiation is the process of _____ _____ to

   _____ _____.

2. A good deal in negotiation is one in which
   _____ is achieved.

3. The two main types of negotiation are:

   a. _____

   b. _____

4. Our basic interests in a negotiation have to do with our

   _____.

5. Many of us have a negative attitude toward negotiation
   because we perceive it as a _____. We
   can overcome this negativity by perceiving negotiation as a

   _____.

Chapter *Two*

Profile of a Negotiator

Chapter Objective

▶ Develop the 10 traits of a successful negotiator.

The best negotiators I know exhibit 10 key attributes that stand out over and above their individual personalities:

1. Developing negotiation consciousness

2. Listening well

3. Having high aspirations

4. Being a detective—asking questions

5. Having patience

6. Maintaining flexible assumptions

7. Focusing on satisfaction

8. Taking risks

9. Solving Problems

10. Being willing to walk away

While attention to these 10 traits will not guarantee your success at negotiating, you will not be successful without them.

The 10 Traits of a Successful Negotiator

Trait 1: Developing Negotiation Consciousness

Every successful negotiator I know proceeds from the assumption that everything is negotiable. Successful negotiators are assertive, and they challenge everything. (I use the word *challenge* instead of *question* because *challenge* is stronger and more dynamic.) I call this trait *negotiation consciousness*.

2

◆ *Challenge* means not taking things at face value. It means thinking for yourself. You must be able to make up your own mind, as opposed to believing everything you are told. On a practical level, this means you have the right to question the asking price of that new car. It also means you have an obligation to question everything you read in the newspaper or hear on CNN. You cannot negotiate unless you are willing to challenge the validity of the opposing position.

> **You cannot negotiate unless you are willing to challenge the validity of the opposing position.**

◆ There is a difference between being assertive and being aggressive. You are assertive when you take care of your own interests while maintaining respect for the interests of others. When you take care of your own interests with a lack of regard for other people's interests, you are aggressive. Being assertive is part of negotiation consciousness.

Assertiveness Training Tips

1. **Ask.**
   Get into the habit of asking for what you want. After all, the worst thing that can happen is that someone will say no. And when you ask, be persistent. Don't take no for an answer. Observe how children will continue to ask for what they want even though their parents say, "No, you can't have that."

2. **Eliminate negative self-talk.**
   Self-awareness is the key. Every time you become aware that your inner voice is telling you not to be assertive, give yourself a pat on the back. Substitute a positive thought for the negative one. "I have a good chance of getting what I want if I ask for it" is more productive than "They'll never say yes."

3. **Practice expressing your feelings without anxiety or anger.**
   Let people know how you feel. A good way to do this is to practice "I" statements. For example, instead of saying, "You shouldn't do that," try substituting, "I don't feel comfortable when you do that."

Let people know how you feel.

4. **Learn how to say no.**
   In other words, set limits. If you perceive yourself as a separate human being, you can establish your boundaries. Don't permit other people to step over those boundaries. This is how we learn to withstand intimidation. "I'm sorry, but I'm really not interested in buying a car today, thank you."

Take a Moment

Instead of being assertive and asking for what we want, we say things to ourselves, such as, "It isn't done" or "They'll say no." List five areas in your life in which you could be more assertive and take better care of yourself. For each area, describe exactly where you feel you have not been assertive enough. Identify statements and behaviors that you would like to change. Then write down the things you can do to be more assertive in each area.

1. _____

_____

2. _____

_____

3. _____

_____

4. _____

_____

5. _____

_____

Trait 2: Listening Well

After negotiation consciousness, listening well is the most important quality for negotiators. People will tell you everything you need to know. All you have to do is listen. We will examine techniques for effective listening in Chapter 6.

Trait 3: Having High Aspirations

When I was in Marine Corps boot camp, I had trouble jumping over a large ditch. (I kept winding up in the ditch instead of over the ditch.) My buddy said, "Ed, instead of focusing down at the ditch, look straight ahead of you—focus your attention way past the ditch." I made it.

A divorced woman friend once said to me, "I realize at my age, I'll never get married again." I thought to myself, "She's right! With an attitude like that, she'll never get married."

If you expect less, you're likely to get less.

If you expect less, you're likely to get less. If you expect a lot, you stand a better chance of making it come true. Successful negotiators are optimists. They have high aspirations. Aim beyond the ditch.

Take a Moment

Select an upcoming negotiation. What are your aspirations?

_____

_____

_____

_____

Trait 4: Being a Detective: Asking Questions

Think of all the movie detectives you've seen, from Sherlock Holmes to Inspector Clousseau to Columbo. What do they all have in common? They ask a lot of questions. Negotiators do the same thing. Negotiators always probe for information. As we will see in Chapter 3, gathering information is vital to your case.

Trait 5: Having Patience

Your worst enemy is that little voice inside your head that keeps saying, "Make the deal and get it over with!" Have you ever been presented with a wonderful proposition and then told that you must decide right away or else you will lose your opportunity? "This offer is good today only." If you can't act with restraint, don't act at all.

In our culture, everybody is in a hurry. If you are patient, you will force me to give in as my anxiety level rises.

Unfortunately, this is not easy for many Americans. Other cultures have a better understanding of the value of patience. One of my handball partners used to live in Japan. His health club in Tokyo had only one handball court for the use of 30 players. When he described to me how the Japanese players would gladly wait for an hour or more to get on the court, we both laughed because we know how impatiently Americans will behave under similar circumstances.

Businesspeople in other countries deliberately prolong negotiations in the knowledge that Americans will give in to the pressure of time. A client of mine once spent eight months in Taiwan to conclude an agreement which he said would have taken less than a week in Houston.

Whoever is more flexible about time has the advantage in a negotiation. Patience gives you the opportunity to think things through. Your patience can be devastating to the other side if they are in a hurry.

> **Whoever is more flexible about time has the advantage in a negotiation.**

Patience Questionnaire

Sometimes people are impatient—they don't realize that they are in the midst of a negotiation. Describe two situations where you rushed to a decision:

1. _____

_____

_____

2. _____

_____

_____

Now that you understand that these situations are actually negotiations, how could you have handled them differently?

1. _____

_____

_____

2. _____

_____

_____

Trait 6: Maintaining Flexible Assumptions

Be flexible—your assumptions may be incorrect. As part of the planning process, you will want to make assumptions about the other negotiator. What is their goal? What options do they have? However, experienced negotiators understand that the most carefully thought-out assumptions may not be validated by the facts. Be prepared to adjust your assumptions as new facts come to light during a negotiation. Some of the rigid assumptions we make are:

2

> **Be prepared to adjust your assumptions as new facts come to light during a negotiation.**

◆ **"I don't have a chance—they hold all the cards!"**
People often make the mistake of assuming that the other side has all the power in a negotiation. Instead of focusing on how tough the situation appears from our perspective, the antidote to this dangerous kind of assumption is to focus on the reasons why the other side needs to reach an agreement. "They need me as much as I need them."

◆ **"Our clients will never accept this price increase."**
Many salespeople will take the side of their customers on the issue of price in order to avoid confronting them with a price increase. Why? Because of the fear of rejection. Actually, I have discovered that none of us has a crystal ball. We can't find out how a customer will respond to a price increase unless we ask them. They may be more amenable to the new price than we suppose. "They will accept my price increase if I can provide reasonable justification."

◆ **"Our vendors will never lower their prices."**
Buyers underestimate their vendor's desire to make the sale. As I mentioned earlier, successful negotiators are optimists. They assume that the glass is half full, not half empty. "They may be willing to lower their price in order to get our business."

◆ **"The buyer doesn't need me—I'd better drop my price right away."**
This reflects the tendency of sellers—and negotiators in general—to focus on their own pressure while ignoring the pressure on the other side. "The buyer will be worse off without my product."

Take a Moment

Think of an upcoming negotiation. What are some of the assumptions that may cause you problems?

1. _____
   _____

2. _____
   _____

3. _____
   _____

4. _____
   _____

5. _____
   _____

How could you change each of these assumptions to be more positive?

1. _____
   _____

2. _____
   _____

3. _____
   _____

4. _____
   _____

5. _____
   _____

Trait 7: Focusing on Satisfaction

Experienced negotiators always ask, "How can I help the other negotiator feel satisfied?" They understand that they can get what they need from the other negotiator as long as the other negotiator feels that their basic needs have been fulfilled. More on satisfaction in Chapter 4.

Trait 8: Taking Risks

The willingness to challenge everything is a form of risk taking. Implied in the concept of negotiation consciousness is the practice of taking reasonable risks. Successful negotiators take more risks than the average person.

Taking risks can involve asking for more than you think you can get. It can involve giving the other side an ultimatum. Or it can mean the willingness to be theatrical.

For example, how do you feel when someone gets emotional in a negotiation? Does it throw you off balance? Good negotiators are good actors. They are not afraid to risk adding a little controlled pizazz to their presentation. (Remember Khrushchev banging his shoe at the UN?) Examples:

- Crying
- Laughing
- Yelling
- Being silent
- Flinching (What!)
- Walking out

Risk taking is part of negotiation as it is part of life.

Take a Moment

Select an upcoming negotiation and answer these two questions:

1. How much risk am I willing to take in this negotiation?

   _____

2. If I take a risk and lose the deal, what options/ alternatives do I have? Do I have a "Plan B"?

   _____

Trait 9: Solving Problems

Successful negotiators focus on solving the problem, not on people or personalities. Although they may act hurt, successful negotiators never allow their personal feelings to interfere with the realization of their goals. They don't take things personally. I can recall an eight-hour screaming match with a client that ended in our going out for a pleasant dinner together. If we had taken all the screaming and posturing seriously, we never would have been able to reach an agreement. As we will see in Chapter 6, focusing on solving the problem is the road to win-win negotiation.

Trait 10: Being Willing to Walk Away

Last but not least, we come to **Brodow's Law:** Always be willing to walk away! In other words, never negotiate without options. Experienced negotiators leave room for "Plan B," their escape hatch. If they depend too much on the positive outcome of a negotiation, they lose their ability to say no.

A friend of mine paid full price for a new car because she refused to say to herself, "If I can't buy this car at the price I want, then I'll buy something else." When you walk into a negotiation with your tongue hanging out, you send a message to the other side that says: "Take me, I'm yours!"

Always be willing to walk away!

I am often asked, "Ed, if you could give me one piece of advice about negotiating, what would it be?" My answer, without hesitation, is: "Always be willing to walk away!"

Successful negotiators understand that certain behavior patterns work best. They are assertive and they challenge everything. They maintain high aspirations. Their assumptions are positive and flexible. They are patient.

They work at being good listeners and good detectives—they ask a lot of questions. They take risks but don't take things personally—they focus on solving the problem. And they focus on satisfaction—they know that satisfied people make better negotiating partners.

Self-Check: Chapter 2 Review
Your Negotiation Quotient

Rate yourself on each of the 10 traits:

		Excellent				Needs Work
1.	Developing negotiation consciousness	5	4	3	2	1
2.	Listening well	5	4	3	2	1
3.	Having high aspirations	5	4	3	2	1
4.	Being a detective: Asking questions	5	4	3	2	1
5.	Having patience	5	4	3	2	1
6.	Maintaining flexible assumptions	5	4	3	2	1
7.	Focusing on satisfaction	5	4	3	2	1
8.	Taking risks	5	4	3	2	1
9.	Solving problems	5	4	3	2	1
10.	Being willing to walk away	5	4	3	2	1

How did you do? You have an opportunity to work on your weak areas in your next negotiation. For example, if you rate yourself as needing work on developing negotiation consciousness, plan to be more assertive. If you lag when it comes to asking perceptive questions, set yourself the goal of becoming a better detective.

The areas I need to focus on are:

1. _____

2. _____

3. _____

Chapter *Three*

Preparing for a Negotiation

Chapter Objectives

▶ Set targets for the results of your negotiation.

▶ Gather information to help you negotiate.

▶ Develop a feeling of power in a negotiation.

▶ Pick a suitable location for your negotiation.

▶ Decide whether to negotiate as an individual or as a team.

▶ Rehearse the negotiation.

A negotiation is not unlike a stage play. The director of a play must analyze the script, select and rehearse the cast, and supervise the set construction. The producer must provide the financial backing, hire a theater, and organize the marketing effort. The actors must learn their lines and develop their interpretation of the material. Without adequate preparation, the whole stack of cards will collapse.

In your negotiations, you are the producer, the director, and the cast. Your preparation must be so thorough that you can relax in the knowledge that you are ready for anything that may occur. To do this, you need to:

◆ Set targets for the results of your negotiation.

◆ Gather information to help you negotiate.

◆ Develop a feeling of power in a negotiation.

◆ Pick a suitable location for your negotiation.

◆ Decide whether to negotiate as an individual or as a team.

◆ Rehearse the negotiation.

Setting Targets

We established in Chapter 2 that good negotiators have high aspirations. To be effective, our aspirations must be specific. We can't go far unless we know exactly where we are going. Targets provide us with a road map.

In order to understand where we are going in a negotiation, we must be aware of three specific targets:

1. **Maximum position**
   The best result we realistically can attain in the negotiation. If everything goes perfectly, this is the optimum. "Pie in the sky."

2. **Goal**
   The result we'll be satisfied to achieve. Our goal is not what we'd like to have—it's what we'll be content with. Most of us will settle for something less than the optimum and still be happy. We want a Mercedes, but we're happy with a Honda. We might settle for something less than our goal, but only under pressure.

3. **Minimum position (also called our bottom line)**
   The worst outcome we will accept under pressure in order to make a deal. We're not entirely satisfied—it's not our goal—but it's better than nothing. Any worse than this and we will walk away.

Your *maximum* gives you guidance for your opening demand. You can begin the negotiation with an effort to get the best possible outcome. If you want to follow the advice given in Chapter 4 about opening with an extreme position, the *maximum* shows you the parameters for that opening. Your bottom line warns you that this is where you will draw the line. Anything less than your bottom line will be unacceptable. Once you know your *bottom line*, you won't be goaded or tricked into accepting the unacceptable. Your *goal* establishes your level of satisfaction. This is what you are striving for.

Your *goal* establishes your level of satisfaction. This is what you are striving for.

For Example . . .

■ Let's take the sale of your house as an example. You put it on the market at $300,000, which is the maximum—the most you think it could sell for. You would be overjoyed to sell it for $300,000. However, you will be quite satisfied if the house goes for $280,000. This is your goal. Anything less than $280,000 and you will be unhappy. However, if the house isn't sold after three months, you will accept $260,000—your bottom line. It won't make you happy, but you'll accept it just to unload the house.

What are your targets?

Bottom Line:
Minimum acceptable.

Goal: What you'll be
satisfied with.

Maximum Position:
The best you could
possibly attain.

Your GOAL = What you'll be satisfied with.

Take a Moment

Select an upcoming negotiation. Write down your:

1. Maximum position:

_____

_____

2. Goal:

_____

_____

3. Minimum position (bottom line):

_____

_____

Once you have written down your positions, you know where you want to steer the negotiation. Now you are ready to begin collecting information.

3

Gathering Information

One of your
main tasks as
a negotiator is
probing for
information.

One of your main tasks as a negotiator, as we discussed in Chapter 2, is acting like a detective and probing for information. You must acquire information about yourself, and then about the other side.

Information About Yourself

◆ **What are your targets?**
1. Maximum
2. Goal
3. Bottom line

◆ **What is your position vs. your needs?**
Make sure that you are able to distinguish between your position and your basic interests (see Chapter 1). Your targets should reflect your true needs in the negotiation.

◆ **What is your starting point?**
Where do you intend to open in the negotiation? The nature of your relationship with the other side will influence your starting demand. In an adversarial situation, you probably will want to open with an extreme position that is closer to the maximum (see "Make Concessions Wisely" in Chapter 4). For example, when buying a new car with a sticker price of $20,000, a lower opening offer of $16,000 will help you achieve your goal of paying no more than $18,000—better than a higher opening offer of, say, $17,500. You generally are better off leaving yourself more room to maneuver. On the other hand, if you have progressed to a cooperative relationship, you may decide that your opening position will correspond more closely to your goal.

◆ **What concessions are you willing to make?**
Make a list in advance of potential concessions. List the items you are willing to give up. Prioritize them. List the items you will not give up. If this is done prior to the negotiation, the chance of making a mistake is reduced considerably.

◆ **What are your options in the negotiation?**
If you don't make a deal, what else can you do? Remember Brodow's Law: Always be willing to walk away. It is easier to project a cavalier attitude if you understand your options. If you don't need to make the deal, you will appear stronger. For example, before buying a new car, make a list of other dealerships you could buy from and other cars you would consider substituting for the one you are looking at now.

◆ **What are your strengths in the negotiation?**
Don't take them for granted. Write them down. This will help you to feel powerful. For example, if you are selling your house, write down all the benefits that will accrue to the buyer. Write down your lack of urgency in selling the house. Write down the fact that several buyers are making offers for you to choose from.

◆ **What are your deadlines?**
List the deadlines in your negotiation. Who created them? If you created them yourself, can you change them?

3

> **Most mistakes
> are made
> under the
> pressure of a
> deadline.**

Most deals are consummated at the last minute. Most mistakes are made under the pressure of a deadline. It is important to be able to make decisions without time pressure.

It's fine if you can impose a deadline on the other side, but don't let them do it to you.

Information About the Other Side

The time to begin gathering information about the other side is far in advance of the actual meeting we call "the negotiation." It is easier to obtain information about your opposite numbers prior to the negotiation. They will be less guarded.

Potential sources of information about the other side in an upcoming negotiation are:

◆ The negotiator(s) for the other side.

◆ The negotiator's secretary.

◆ Someone else in the other company.

◆ Someone who has done business with the other company.

◆ Published information about the other company.

Information You Will Need

◆ **What is the other side's pressure?**
Your strength is in direct proportion to the pressure experienced by the other side. If they are under pressure to make a deal, they are more motivated to make concessions to you.

> Remember to look beyond their position to what really is motivating them.

◆ **What are their targets?**
What will satisfy them? It may be less than you assume. Put yourself in their shoes. What is their maximum? goal? minimum?

◆ **What are their needs vs. their position?**
Remember to look beyond their position to what really is motivating them. Your understanding of their basic needs will help you to identify possibilities for mutual satisfaction.

◆ **What are their options?**
You must understand what their alternatives are. They will negotiate differently depending on how many options they perceive are available to them.

◆ **What are their deadlines?**
How can you benefit from these deadlines? Can you impose a deadline?

Information About Industry Standards and Objective Criteria

You should also try to learn whether there are any mutually acceptable standards/objective criteria that can be used to reach an agreement. Agreement can be reached quickly if both sides are willing to accept standards. Standards can include:

♦ **The way things are done in your industry**
Agreement can be reached if both sides accept the "usual" way of doing things. When you buy a television set, the manufacturer includes a warranty. The length of that warranty will be the same for all brands because the industry has accepted that standard. Most buyers accept the standard because they know "everybody else is getting the same treatment."

♦ **The way it was done the last time**
People feel comfortable knowing that the agreement follows a proven formula. My electric bill used to include a mysterious four-dollar charge every month. I was content paying it every month because I had paid it the month before. One day I was jolted out of my complacency, and I called the utility company. It turned out that the four-dollar charge was for garbage collection service which I didn't use (a private firm collected my garbage). All this time I had dutifully paid the four dollars because I had paid it the last time. The precedent gave me a sense of comfort.

♦ **Use of objective criteria**
A buyer and a seller may agree that the seller's prices will escalate in proportion to the rise in the Consumer Price Index. A bank's loan rates are indexed in relation to Treasury Notes or Certificates of Deposit. Automobile insurance premiums are adjusted in accordance with statistics on accident rates in your locality.

> **Agreement can be reached quickly if both sides are willing to accept standards.**

3

Information About the Agenda

Don't forget to create a list of all the items to be discussed in the negotiation.

◆ **Identify the issues.**
Be prepared so that you won't forget something that may be important to you later on. Even if you don't use the agenda as a formal tool during the negotiation, it can serve as a checklist of all the items that are relevant. Think of it as a table of contents.

Don't feel obligated to begin where the other side wants to begin.

◆ **Develop an agenda that reflects your priorities.**
Which issues do you want to deal with first? How much time do you want to allot to each issue? Are there any issues that you feel are outside the scope of this negotiation?

◆ **Don't allow the other side to write the agenda to favor their position.**
Bring in other issues that you feel are important. Be prepared to challenge the priorities represented in their agenda. Don't feel obligated to begin where the other side wants to begin.

Preparation Worksheet

Identify an upcoming negotiation. Gather the information you need:

About yourself:
1. What are your targets?
    - Maximum:
    - Goal:
    - Bottom Line:
2. What are your real needs?
3. What is your starting point?
4. What concessions are you willing to make?
5. What concessions won't you make?
6. What are your options?
7. What are your strengths?
8. What are your deadlines? Are they negotiable?

About the other side:
1. What is their pressure in the negotiation?
2. What are their real needs?
3. What are their options?
4. What is your estimate of their targets?
    - Maximum:
    - Goal:
    - Bottom Line:
5. What are the deadlines for the other side? Can you create one?

About objective criteria:
1. Are there any mutually acceptable standards/criteria you can use to reach agreement?

About the agenda:
1. What are the issues in this negotiation?

3

Developing a Feeling of Power in a Negotiation

Negotiation has strong emotional and psychological undercurrents. In an adversarial negotiation, we think about "psyching out" the other person. We worry about being intimidated by them. The concept of power as it relates to negotiation is an expression of emotional/psychological relationships. We want to feel as powerful as possible so that we have the strength to fulfill our needs. Let's examine how we can create a feeling of confidence.

Definition of Power

Power is the ability to influence the outcome of a negotiation. Power is subjective. You are powerful if you believe you are. If you convey self-confidence to others, they will believe it. So when we speak of power, we really are speaking about self-confidence.

> *Power* is the ability to influence the outcome of a negotiation.

In an adversarial negotiation, you are powerful when you have the self-confidence to demonstrate to the other side that they will be hurt by not agreeing. In a cooperative negotiation, you are powerful when you can convince the other side that— although they have options—they are better off with a deal. Power derives from a number of sources.

Sources of Your Negotiating Strength

◆ **Having options**
Your ability and willingness to walk away from the negotiation place you in a very powerful position. If you are negotiating with a Ford dealer, your willingness to walk across the street and buy a Chevrolet gives you power.

◆ **Remaining patient**
Your willingness to outwait the other negotiator gives you power. As we saw in Chapter 2, whoever is more flexible about time has the advantage.

◆ **Processing information**
As we saw earlier in this chapter, "Information is power."
That's why we have the CIA. A substantial part of your job
as a negotiator involves the collection of information.

◆ **Demonstrating commitment**
The more committed you are to your objectives, the more
powerful you will appear in a negotiation. Gandhi was a
wonderful example of this kind of commitment. For all
practical purposes, he had no power over the British in
India. However, Gandhi's commitment to his course of
action invested him with remarkable power.

The more commitment you can get from the other
negotiator about your position, the more powerful you
become. Solicit agreement. This is why sellers always try to
get buyers to agree that they love the product.

The more time and effort you can get the other negotiator to
commit, the bigger their stake in concluding an agreement.
A friend of mine always spends at least four hours when he
buys a car. He knows that the stakes are much higher for the
salesperson who has devoted so much time to a customer.

◆ **Showing persistence**
This means hanging in there and not giving up just because
someone says "no." Children are very good at this. Watch
them.

◆ **Taking risks**
As we discussed in Chapter 2, taking reasonable risks based
upon reliable information will boost your power. We are all
familiar with the saying, "Nothing ventured, nothing
gained."

3

> **The more time
> and effort you
> can get
> the other
> negotiator to
> commit, the
> bigger their
> stake in
> concluding an
> agreement.**

◆ **Having legitimacy**
You have power if your position is supported by authority.

- Anything in writing has legitimacy.

- Whatever is the norm in your industry has legitimacy.

- The way it was done the last time has legitimacy.

- If the experts say it is so, they bestow legitimacy.

Find ways of sprinkling a dose of legitimacy onto your position.

◆ **Showing weakness**
We may possess power but not be able to use it. The Peter Sellers comedy, *The Mouse That Roared,* featured a small country whose objective was to lose a war with the United States in order to receive foreign aid. Sometimes weakness can be your source of power.

- "Help me." You admit that you're weak and ask the other negotiator to help you. "I really don't understand this. Can you help me?"

- Play dumb. Instead of showing them how smart you are, let them be smart and come up with the answers. This strategy capitalizes on the ego of other negotiators. Let's face it, we all love to show off.

Your power lies in the self-confidence you develop by respecting these sources of strength.

Picking a Suitable Location for the Negotiation

The location of a negotiation can affect the nature of the outcome. There are advantages to holding the proceedings at home and advantages to traveling to the other team's ballpark.

> **The location of a negotiation can affect the nature of the outcome.**

Your Place—Advantages

◆ You have access to your decision makers and facilities. You can call in experts as needed. Additional information is readily at hand. If unexpected issues are raised, senior management can be called in.

◆ You have more control over the other side. It's more difficult for them to create interruptions or distractions. The meeting room and dining arrangements can be managed to your benefit.

◆ You have the psychological advantage of being in your home ballpark. As professional ball players can attest, being in familiar territory is comforting.

Their Place—Advantages

◆ You can use limited authority. "I don't have the authority to do that." This is a technique for making fewer concessions (see Chapters 4 and 5). If you are asked for concessions that you are not prepared to give, you may politely decline due to the absence of key decision makers. (It's tough to use this technique if your decision makers are just down the corridor.)

◆ You have access to their decision makers. They are prevented from using limited authority to refuse your request for concessions.

◆ They may feel more comfortable at home, and hence more willing to consider your perspective.

A Neutral Place—Advantages

Sometimes it's a good idea to relax the other negotiators by getting away from a formal business environment. I recall one difficult sale that I thought we'd never close because of constant interruptions in the buyer's office. The buyer's phone kept ringing. His employees would march in and out, destroying the flow of our negotiations. We couldn't get his attention long enough to consummate a deal. We finally took him to his favorite restaurant where the sale was closed over dessert.

Deciding Whether to Negotiate as an Individual or as a Team

One of the major decisions in many negotiations revolves around the number of negotiators. As in the decision of where to locate the negotiation, there are pros and cons in determining how many of you there should be.

Advantages of an Individual Negotiator

An individual
can often make
decisions
easier and
faster than a
committee.

◆ An individual can often make decisions easier and faster than a committee. A single negotiator doesn't need to consult with partners, a process that can be very time-consuming and which often results in an internal deadlock.

◆ An individual can use limited authority as the means of not giving concessions. You can refuse a request simply by informing the other side that you don't have the authority to give that concession.

◆ Your position won't be weakened by differences of opinion. The other side can't try to create disagreement among team members.

Advantages of a Negotiation Team

◆ Teams can avoid making quick decisions. Individuals often make mistakes that would never occur with team members present. Remember that patience is a virtue.

◆ Teams can benefit from a pooling of judgments. Two (or more) heads are better than one. Each team member can make a unique contribution.

◆ There is strength in numbers. A team is often perceived as more powerful than an individual. And we are better risk takers when we can share the risk with partners.

◆ With a team, you can bring in experts. Experts add to your credibility.

◆ There is less pressure on each individual member of the team. When you negotiate by yourself, there is little or no time to sit back and think. Team members can take turns at the helm while the others listen and observe.

3

A team is often perceived as more powerful than an individual.

43

Rehearsing the Negotiation

Conduct a practice negotiation before you negotiate with the other side.

A stage production could not take place without rehearsal. A negotiation should be no different. Conduct a practice negotiation before you negotiate with the other side. Ask colleagues to assume the roles of the people you actually will be negotiating with. This role-playing can be critical in helping you to:

◆ **Anticipate the other side's strategies and tactics.**
When your colleagues get into their roles, they will begin to uncover the approach that you will be faced with in the actual negotiation.

◆ **Understand the other side's position and interests.**
You will make a tremendous impression with the insights you gain during the rehearsal.

◆ **Prepare your own strategies and tactics.**
Your preparation will be much easier once you gain a better understanding of the issues in the negotiation.

Chapter 3 has exposed you to the basic steps you need to follow in preparation for a negotiation. Chapter 4 will introduce you to some of the strategies you need to be aware of during the negotiation.

Self-Check: Chapter 3 Review

Answers to these questions appear on page 95.

1. Define goal:

    _____

    _____

2. Define bottom line:

    _____

    _____

3. What four types of information should you gather before you begin negotiating?

    a. _____

    b. _____

    c. _____

    d. _____

4. List three sources of negotiation power.

    a. _____

    b. _____

    c. _____

5. The best place for you to conduct your next negotiation is_____ for the following reasons:

    _____

    _____

6. Who are the people in your organization that can help you rehearse your next negotiation?

    _____

Chapter *Four*

Strategies for Adversarial Negotiating

Chapter Objective

▶ Master five strategies to help you succeed in adversarial negotiation situations.

Even though you may regard yourself as an advocate of win-win negotiation, the person or team with whom you negotiate may engage in adversarial negotiation. This type of competitive situation often creates feelings of anxiety for negotiators. Don't let fear keep you from negotiating effectively! Believe it or not, you can successfully handle this type of negotiation and possibly even learn to enjoy it. Five strategies that will help you negotiate successfully in an adversarial situation are:

◆ Help the other side feel satisfied with the negotiation results.

◆ Don't reveal too much information.

◆ Lower the other side's expectations.

◆ Make concessions wisely.

◆ Be willing to walk away.

Strategy 1: Help the Other Side Feel Satisfied

In the preceding chapters, I have stressed the importance of satisfaction in the negotiation process. Helping other negotiators to feel satisfied is a smart way to get what we want from them.

Here are some key points for giving satisfaction:

◆ Remember to focus on their real interests as opposed to their stated position. The people you negotiate with will practically fall over when they realize that you understand their needs. As we will discover in Chapter 6, the way to develop trust in a negotiation is by demonstrating that you appreciate the other side's needs. Even in the most adversarial negotiation, you must give them a sense that their basic interests are being fulfilled.

◆ How you behave with other negotiators is more important than the concessions you make. In fact, you can satisfy them without actually giving up a substantial concession. Satisfaction can be created by:

1. **Giving them a meaningful explanation.**
   The worst feeling in a negotiation is the one that screams, "You are being taken advantage of!" By giving straightforward explanations for your inability or unwillingness to give in, you help the other negotiator to rationalize your behavior. You want them to be thinking, "Okay, I don't like this, but I can understand their reasons for taking this approach."

   Suppose you are negotiating with your teenage son and/or daughter for a raise in their allowance. They want the raise and you don't. You can help them to accept your decision by pointing out that there will be no raise until you pay off the recent heavy expenses for their dental work. They won't get the raise, but they will walk away with a sense that you care for them.

> To develop trust in a negotiation, demonstrate that you appreciate the other side's needs.

4

2. **Giving them a minor concession.**
   We all place different values on things. Something that may be insignificant to you may be very meaningful to the other negotiator. The fact that you are giving up anything at all can create a feeling of satisfaction.

   Let's say you are not authorized to give one of your employees the salary increase he or she was expecting. Instead, you give out a new title and more responsibility. The new title doesn't cost you anything, but he or she experiences satisfaction because it means a lot.

3. **Stroking their egos.**
   People love to be validated. By telling a valued employee how much you appreciate his or her work, you give satisfaction without giving the raise that never got approved.

4. **Giving them an ultimatum.**
   This is the best you can do, you've gone to your limit, and you're prepared to walk away. How does this help the other negotiator to feel satisfied? (See Chapter 5 for the answer.)

5. **Listening to them.**
   Sometimes all we want is someone who will pay attention to us. Try this with your children. In his autobiography, actor Kirk Douglas describes how as a child he threw a cup of scalding hot tea in his father's face. His father picked young Kirk up and threw him across the room. Mr. Douglas admits that he was delighted at the attention he received.

   Satisfaction can come from from the simple act of listening.

Sometimes all we want is someone who will pay attention to us.

Take a Moment

List some of the ways you can impart a sense of
satisfaction to the other person in an upcoming negotiation.

1. _____

_____

2. _____

_____

3. _____

_____

4

Strategy 2: Don't Reveal Too Much Information

Everything you say or do in a negotiation has some effect on the
other negotiator's aspirations. They will expect more or they will
expect less depending on how you behave during the
negotiation. In a competitive negotiation, you will raise their
expectations if you disclose information that is damaging to
your position.

In point of fact, it is not necessary for you to disclose everything
you know to the other negotiator. It is often suicide. Making
them aware of your pressure in the negotiation will cause them
to offer you fewer concessions and expect more concessions
from you.

For example, sellers generally should not disclose their cost and
profit data to their buyers. A buyer may decide that the seller's
profit is excessive. If a buyer asks for a price breakdown, the
seller can respond that such information is proprietary.

> Everything you
> say or do in a
> negotiation has
> some effect
> on the other
> negotiator's
> aspirations.

Take a Moment

You are at the car dealership getting ready to buy a new car. List some things you could say (but which you won't after reading this book) that would raise the dealer's expectations. (Suggestions appear on page 95.)

_____

_____

_____

_____

_____

_____

_____

Strategy 3: Lower the Other Side's Expectations

Once again, everything you say or do in a negotiation has some effect on the other negotiator's aspirations. Your position is greatly improved if you can send the other negotiator a message that you don't need them. Their expectations will go down. If they expect to get less, you will wind up getting more.

If they expect to get less, you will wind up getting more.

Take a Moment

You are at the car dealership buying that new car. What can you say or do to lower the expectations of the dealer? (Answers appear on page 96.)

_____

_____

_____

_____

_____

_____

_____

_____

4

It is important to be able to distinguish between the kinds of statements you want to make as opposed to those you want to avoid. Seek to lower their expectations, not raise them!

Strategy 4: Make Concessions Wisely

No opening is too extreme if you can provide some good reasons to justify it.

Concessions constitute a critical component of the negotiation process. We all make them. However, the important thing is not what concessions we make but how we make them. The process is crucial to giving satisfaction. Ironically, you can give someone the moon and they may not feel satisfied. Yet, if you give them less but do it properly, they will thank you for it. Here are some of the rules for making concessions in an adversarial negotiation:

Open with an Extreme Position

Buyers should open with a low offer. Sellers should open with a high demand. This leaves you room to give something away. When you do this, the other negotiator feels satisfied because it allows them to obtain a concession from you. How extreme should your opening be? No opening is too extreme if you can provide some good reasons to justify it.

For example, a seller hoping to receive $250,000 (their goal) for their house might put it on the market at $300,000 (their maximum). The couple purchasing the house for $275,000 will tell their friends that they "stole" the house because they negotiated $25,000 off of the listing price.

At the same time that you are giving satisfaction, you will also lower the expectations of the other negotiator. In the last example, the buyer's expectation of getting the house for $250,000 is lowered by the seller's $300,000 asking price. From the other perspective, if the buyer's opening offer to the seller is $225,000, the seller's expectation of getting $300,000 is lowered. The seller may be more willing to sell their house at a lower price than they originally hoped for.

In a corporate setting, consider an aircraft manufacturer being pressured by a customer for delivery of a new airplane. Although the manufacturer anticipates a 12-month turnaround, the customer is told that delivery will be in 18 months. If the customer negotiates and wins a 14-month delivery date, they will be bragging about their negotiating prowess. In reality, the manufacturer left room to negotiate by opening with an extreme position (18 months).

Make Small Concessions

A small concession helps the other negotiator feel satisfied because they think they've pushed you to your bottom line. When a seller tells a buyer, "I can only discount my product 2 percent," the buyer senses that the seller really doesn't have much room to maneuver.

A large concession, on the other hand, conveys a message of weakness. If the seller offers a 40 percent discount, the buyer begins to suspect that there may be something wrong with the product (otherwise the seller wouldn't be so generous). I am reminded of Britain's huge concession to Germany immediately prior to World War II. Prime Minister Neville Chamberlain agreed to Germany's takeover of Czechoslovakia in return for Hitler's promise not to attack anybody else. All it did was raise Hitler's aspirations and encourage him to attack Poland. If Britain had stood its ground and warned Hitler to back off, our history books might read differently.

4

A small concession helps the other negotiator feel satisfied.

Vary the Size of Your Concessions

If your concessions fall into a pattern, the other negotiator will think you have a bottomless well of things to give away.

Let's say you list your house for sale at $300,000. After receiving a buyer's offer of $250,000, you drop your price to $290,000. The buyer doesn't bite, so you drop your price to $280,000. The buyer still doesn't bite, so you drop your price to $270,000. Can you see the pattern emerging? If the buyer sees you make concession after concession of $10,000, they will expect more $10,000 concessions. Avoid this kind of pattern.

The size of your concessions should decrease. After dropping your price $10,000 (from $300,000 to $290,000), your next move might be a concession of only $5,000 (down to $285,000), then a concession of $2,000 (down to $283,000). At this point, the buyer ought to be getting the message that your bottom line is somewhere in the low $280s. They will be satisfied paying that amount.

Don't Make the First Move

The best way to find out if the other negotiator's aspirations are low is to induce them to open first. They may surprise you. You were expecting a tough demand . . . and you discover that they weren't expecting as much as you thought.

Do you remember the story of my friend, the professional speaker, who undercut his fee? Suppose, instead of revealing his fee up front, he asked his client, "How much do you have in your budget?" The client might have disclosed a budget that exceeded my friend's full fee. Unfortunately, he never found out because he didn't ask.

> **The best way to find out if the other negotiator's aspirations are low is to induce them to open first.**

Don't Accept the First Offer

If you accept the first offer immediately, the other negotiator will think that they could have done better (it was too easy). An effective way to create a sense of satisfaction is by rejecting the first offer, even though it may be attractive. The other side will feel more satisfied—even though they wind up with less—if they think that they have pushed you as far as you are prepared to go.

Imagine this hypothetical negotiation: A conglomerate is selling one of its divisions to another conglomerate. The seller's asking price is $1 billion. The negotiator for the buyer says, "We can only offer you $900 million." The seller immediately replies, "Okay, we'll take it." What do you suppose is going through the mind of the buyer at this point? "Ooops, we offered too much!"

In this example, the seller might reply to the buyer's $900 million offer with, "We won't take less than $950 million." If they eventually settle at $930 million, the buyer will be more satisfied than they would have been at $900 million. Why? Because the buyer thinks, "We really pushed them to their limit."

Avoid Reciprocal Concessions

Your concessions can be smaller than the ones you receive. You don't have to match the other negotiator dollar for dollar.

In the conglomerate example, suppose the buyer offers $600 million. In response, the seller makes a concession of $100 million, coming down from $1 billion to $900 million. The buyer is not obligated to offer a reciprocal concession, i.e., going from $600 million to $700 million. The buyer may want to raise their offer by only $50 million, to $650 million.

> **If you accept the first offer immediately, the other negotiator will think that they could have done better.**

4

Make Some Straw Demands

Ask for some
things you
don't really
care about or
think you'll
get.

Ask for some things you don't really care about or think you'll get. You can concede these for others you do care about. Try this during your next car purchase: The dealer has the car you want equipped with leather seats that you really like but don't want to pay for. Tell the dealer that you want the leather seats at no charge and you want a fancy stereo system (your straw demand) installed at no charge. You can surrender your demand for the stereo in return for the leather seats.

Enter the Negotiation with Limited Authority to Make the Deal

"I don't have the authority to give that concession." This is a wonderful way to avoid making concessions. If the other negotiator has time constraints, as they so often do, they probably will not want you to go through the time-consuming process of getting the necessary authority.

Everyone's favorite example of the use of limited authority seems to be at the car dealer—when your salesperson says, "I can't accept your offer without getting my manager's approval."

If you have any doubts about whether this technique is effective, try negotiating with the attendant in a parking garage. If the parking fee is 10 dollars, offer five. They will have no problem letting you know that they don't have the authority to discount the fee. And good luck trying to find out who does have the authority!

Whenever You Give Something Away, Get Something in Return

Never make unilateral concessions. Always tie a string: "I'll do this if you do that."

When you give a concession to people, it is human nature for them to be grateful. Their gratitude represents an opportunity to get something back from them. A wonderful way to create satisfaction is to say, "Okay, you can have what you want if I can have what I want." If a colleague at work asks you for a special report, make it contingent upon receiving the loan of that person's secretary. When you agree to pay full price for a new personal computer, make it contingent upon the inclusion of some free software.

> **When you give a concession to people, it is human nature for them to be grateful.**

4

Make Minor Concessions

They may be minor to you but major to the other negotiator. Remember that we place different values on things. As we discussed earlier in this chapter, something that may not be important to you may be very meaningful to the other negotiator. Satisfaction may derive from the very idea that you are giving something up.

Make the Other Side Work for Concessions

Asking for something in return for your concessions is another way of making them earn what they get.

People have a greater appreciation of what they receive if they have to work for it. And they will be discouraged from asking for more. The corollary is that if people get what they want too easily, they tend to take it for granted.

Don't just give in when someone asks you for a concession. Make them earn it. For example, don't accept the first offer—force the other negotiator to work harder for an agreement. Asking for something in return for your concessions is another way of making them earn what they get.

Try this with your children: If your child asks for money to see a movie, and you say yes, they probably will be encouraged by your lack of objections and will ask for more money. However, if you make it difficult for the child to receive the money—by demanding that they earn it by washing the dishes, for example—they will have a greater appreciation of the money they earned and will be discouraged from asking for more.

Don't Split the Difference

When someone asks you to split the difference, they are in effect offering you a concession of half the difference. Hold out for the other half.

You have listed your house for $300,000, and a buyer has offered to pay $260,000. You reject the $260,000 offer. The buyer then says, "Let's split the difference and agree on $280,000." If you stop to think about it, the buyer has just offered to pay you at least $280,000. How much more do you want?

Leave Something on the Table

Let the other negotiator go away thinking they won something. It is always a good idea to leave a little something on the table. Don't make the mistake of pushing them too far, or else they may try to get even.

Take a Moment

Identify an upcoming negotiation.

1. Where will you open? (Have you left yourself room to make concessions?)

   _____

   _____

   _____

2. Make a list of straw demands.

   _____

   _____

   _____

3. Make a list of concessions you are willing to make. What can you ask for in return for making those concessions?

   _____

   _____

   _____

4. Make a list of minor concessions you can offer.

   _____

   _____

   _____

4

Strategy 5: Be Willing to Walk Away

We have examined the importance of being willing to walk away from a negotiation. Your willingness to walk away from a deal can actually foster an agreement:

> **Willingness to walk away from a deal can actually foster an agreement.**

◆ **It may force the other side to compromise.**
I once walked out of a buyer's office after the buyer reneged on a promise to sign a purchase order for the computer I was selling. He literally ran after me, begging me to come back and give him another chance. My willingness to walk out demonstrated to him that he had pushed me too far.

◆ **It provides the other negotiators with ammunition to convince their boss to make the deal on your terms.**
Remember that they may have to justify their concessions. Your willingness to walk away can help them to provide that justification.

◆ **It demonstrates your commitment to your position.**
They may be testing you to see how far you will go. Your willingness to walk will show them.

Sometimes you're better off walking away from a deal. For example, I always ask salespeople, "Will this agreement bring you a profit?" If an agreement will involve mostly aggravation, shouldn't you consider closing the door on it?

In this chapter, we have examined the rules for competitive negotiating. Some of them, such as not revealing too much information, involve basic common sense. Others, notably the guidelines for making concessions, revolve around the principle of creating a sense of satisfaction for the other negotiator. Your knowledge of these concepts will make you a more powerful negotiator. You cannot become a good cooperative negotiator until you fully comprehend the adversarial principles that have been the mainstay of negotiation for most of human history.

Self-Check: Chapter 4 Review

Answers to these questions appear on page 96.

1. List three techniques for helping the other side feel satisfied with the outcome of a negotiation.

    a. _____

    b. _____

    c. _____

2. In an adversarial negotiation, you will raise the other side's expectations if you

    _____

    _____

3. Large concessions convey a message of

    _____.

4. Whenever you give something away, you should

    _____

    _____

5. List three reasons why your willingness to walk away from a negotiation could foster an agreement.

    a. _____

    b. _____

    c. _____

Chapter *Five*

Negotiation Tactics

Chapter Objectives

▶ Recognize common negotiation tactics.

▶ Negotiate wisely over the telephone.

▶ Understand common negotiating styles.

▶ Appreciate differences between U.S. negotiation practices and those of other cultures.

W hat should you do if another negotiator hits you with an emotional outburst? How can you tell if you're negotiating effectively over the telephone? What is your opponent's negotiation style—and how can you deal with it? How do U.S. negotiation practices differ from those of other cultures? These are a few of the questions we'll consider in this chapter.

Common Negotiation Tactics

Many of us lack confidence in our negotiating ability because we feel vulnerable to negotiation tactics. Let's look at a dozen common tactics and what to do about them.

1. **Creating an emotional barrage**
   A person you are negotiating with is so angry that he or she seems out of control. This can be very intimidating. Here are some techniques for dealing with negotiators who hit you with an emotional barrage:

   ◆ Allow them to vent their feelings. Once they do, they will be able to look at the real issue—solving the problem. If you attempt to interrupt them or try to argue with them, they will get angrier. Their immediate need is to express their feelings. All you have to do is listen.

◆ Empathize with them (without agreeing to anything). "Yes. I understand how you feel." This will help to disarm their outburst.

◆ When they calm down, ask them what they really want. "What would you like us to do for you?" You may be surprised to discover that all they wanted was to be heard. They may even apologize for their behavior. If their demands are unacceptable, at least they will be willing to discuss them once the barrage is over.

2. **Lowering expectations**
The other negotiator may try to lower your expectations by saying things that are damaging to your position or by opening with an extreme position. The defense against this tactic is simple—you must recognize what they are doing. Your awareness that they are attempting to lower your expectations will enable you to maintain those expectations in the negotiation.

For example, a home buyer may try to lower the seller's expectations by pointing out the house's shortcomings—real and imagined. "There aren't enough bedrooms, the closet space is insufficient, the ceilings are too high/too low, etc." The buyer is hoping to justify a low offer. The seller's defense against this approach is to concentrate on the house's attributes, which will justify the full listing price.

3. **Giving an ultimatum**
This is my final position, take it or leave it! It may be necessary to use an ultimatum in order to demonstrate your resolve on a particular issue. This tactic actually can help the other negotiator to feel satisfied. If they perceive that they have pushed you as far as possible, they will conclude that they have done the best they can. This enables them to rationalize giving in. Here are some ways to deal with an ultimatum:

◆ Challenge it (call their bluff). They may be testing you. Your willingness to walk away will test their resolve.

◆ Ignore it. Change the focus from the ultimatum to a discussion of the issues.

5

> **It may be necessary to use an ultimatum in order to demonstrate your resolve on a particular issue.**

4. **Telling a sob story**
   "All I can afford is . . ." "All I have in my budget is . . ." The message is that they would like to do business with you, but the price exceeds their budget. This tactic works very well against a seller who is desperate to make a sale. Use these techniques to deal with a sob story:

   ◆ Find out if there are other budgets that can be applied to this project. The budget to which they are referring may be one of several that they can draw from.

   ◆ Challenge it (call their bluff). They may be testing the legitimacy of your price.

   ◆ Offer alternatives. "If you can't afford this car, how about that less expensive model?"

   ◆ Change the payment terms. "If you can't pay cash for this car, how about financing it over five years?"

5. **Putting on the squeeze**
   "You'll have to do better than that!" "Your competitor is offering a better deal." The message is that they would prefer to do business with you, but they can get a better deal elsewhere. This works for the same reason that the sob story works. A desperate seller may be inclined to give in. The danger is that the seller may degrade the quality of the product in order to do better pricewise. Use these methods to deal with a squeeze:

   ◆ Get more information. Find out why you have to do better. And how much better?

   ◆ Resell your product or service. Take the focus off of price and concentrate on features and benefits. By differentiating your product from your competitor's, you can justify the difference in price.

   ◆ Tie a string. Agree to the squeeze on the condition that you receive a concession in return, e.g., double the volume of the purchase.

Agree to the squeeze on the condition that you receive a concession in return.

6. **Taking a nibble**

   After the deal is consummated, they ask you for some additional concessions. Buyers nibble by asking for free engineering assistance or additional product warranty. Sellers nibble by asking for an extension of the delivery date. Here's how to deal with a nibble:

   ◆ Show them a price list—"If you want this, here's the price."

   ◆ Limited authority—"I don't have the authority to give you this."

   ◆ Pretend it's a joke and say no.

   ◆ If you are being nibbled constantly for the same item, include the nibbled item in your price.

   ◆ Hold them to their agreement. "Sorry, we are depending on your promised delivery date."

   > **If you are being nibbled constantly for the same item, include the nibbled item in your price.**

7. **Staging an escalation**

   Before the agreement is consummated, they renege on an important part of the deal to which they already agreed. For example, after your car salesperson agrees to a sale price of $20,000, the sales manager walks in and says, "Sorry, we can't do it for less than $21,500." This tactic works because the buyer has already decided to go ahead with the purchase. Psychologically, the buyer is committed. Here's how to deal with an escalation:

   ◆ Hold them to their original commitment. "You agreed to this. If you made a mistake, that's your problem."

   ◆ Walk out. They may beg you to come back.

8. **Playing good guy/bad guy**

   One negotiator is difficult to deal with, the other is easy. The police use this technique in interrogations. The "bad guy" softens up the subject, who is relieved when the "good guy" shows up. This tactic sometimes works well against an obstinate opponent. How to deal with this tactic: ignore it. When they see it isn't working, they will stop.

5

65

9. **Springing a surprise**
   Some aspect of the negotiation suddenly is changed for the purpose of throwing you off guard. A new negotiator is brought in; new information is introduced; there is a change in behavior (sudden anger, lack of attention). Here's how to deal with this tactic:

   ◆ In case of something new, insist on adequate time to prepare for the new situation. "We will need another month to look into this."

   ◆ In case of changed behavior, ignore it.

10. **Making an assumptive close**
    The other negotiator behaves as though you already have agreed to their position. Remember when credit card companies used to send you credit cards that you never asked for? If you didn't return it, you had a new credit card. My dentist does this if I need a root canal job. He doesn't ask me if I'd like one. He simply schedules the appointment. How can you deal with this tactic? Be assertive (see Chapter 2). Don't allow yourself to be bulldozed. As Nancy Reagan used to advise, "Just say no."

11. **Forcing a delay**
    The other side delays making a decision. You are forced to make a concession because you are operating under a deadline or because you are impatient. This tactic has been used successfully against Americans by negotiators from other countries who are aware of our impatient nature. Remember my client who was forced to spend eight months in Taiwan? Here are some tactics for dealing with a delay:

    ◆ Learn to exercise patience. If you have a deadline, change it.

    ◆ Give them a deadline to meet. "This price is only good until Friday."

Learn to exercise patience. If you have a deadline, change it.

12. **Showing limited authority**

They inform you that they can't give you a concession because they don't have the authority to make a decision. You are in a hurry so you agree to their position. Here are some ways to deal with limited authority:

♦ Challenge their assertion that they don't have authority. They may be bluffing.

♦ Find out who does have the authority—ask to deal with that person.

Take a Moment

Make a list of the tactics that have been used against you in recent negotiations.

How could you have dealt with each of them?

1. _____

_____

2. _____

_____

3. _____

_____

4. _____

_____

5

Negotiating Wisely Over the Telephone

Communication is 90 percent nonverbal. Telephone negotiations present a unique problem because we are limited to the verbal 10 percent. We can't observe each other's body language. Misunderstandings are inevitable. You can protect yourself by following four rules:

1. **Buffer your calls.**
   People who call you have an advantage because they are prepared. You may not be ready when they call. If you take the call, you are asking for trouble. Your lack of preparedness will encourage mistakes. By buffering your calls, you can postpone the discussion until you are ready. Examples of buffers include:

   ◆ Screening by a secretary or receptionist. If you are not prepared to negotiate, don't accept the call. Your secretary can take a message or ask the calling party to try again later.

   ◆ Using voice mail. "I'm sorry I can't take your call. Please leave me a message and I will call you back."

   ◆ Answering your own phone, and postponing the negotiation until you are ready. "Can I call you back in 10 minutes?"

> **The less you talk, the less you are likely to make mistakes.**

2. **Listen more than you speak.**
   You can learn all sorts of useful information while volunteering very little. The less you talk, the less you are likely to make mistakes. I suggest a 70/30 rule. That is, listen 70 percent of the time and speak 30 percent of the time.

3. **Don't be in a hurry to agree.**
   We tend to rush things over the phone. Don't allow that silly little piece of equipment—your telephone—to dictate your priorities. If you're not ready to commit, put it off.

4. **Write a deal memo.**
   Nobody remembers everything that was said during a
   telephone negotiation. After the conversation, write the
   other negotiator a memo stating the items agreed upon. This
   will help you to avoid misunderstandings later on.

**Nobody
remembers
everything
that was
said during
a telephone
negotiation.**

Sample Telephone Deal Memo

```
To:        Ed Brodow
Subject:   Our telephone conversation this
           morning

This will confirm my understanding of our
discussion as follows:

1.   We agreed that telephone negotiations can
     lead to misunderstandings primarily
     because of the absence of nonverbal cues.

2.   You offered to provide me with four rules
     to follow in telephone negotiations.

3.   I agreed to follow those rules.
```

5

Take a Moment

Using your last telephone negotiation as an example, write a deal memo.

To: _____

Subject: _____

_____

_____

_____

_____

_____

_____

Understanding Common Negotiating Styles

Some negotiators exhibit distinctive styles. Some common styles are:

Some negotiators exhibit distinctive styles.

1. **Tough guys**
   They are ego-driven and try to show what great negotiators they are by using threats, bullying, ridicule, and guilt. Stand up to them. You can massage their egos while sending them a message that you don't fold in the face of strong-arm tactics. Gradually lower their expectations.

2. **Nice guys**
   They may act nice, but they can be tougher than the more obvious tough guys. Don't be taken in by all the smiles and glitter. Focus on the issues.

3. **Nitpickers**
   They try your patience by insisting that you go over every last detail. Many buyers are nitpickers because they know it drives salespeople crazy. Learn to be patient. Don't allow them to wear you down.

4. **Absent-minded professors**
   They act like they don't know what they are doing, but don't be fooled. Think of Columbo, the T.V. detective. By acting goofy, he encourages his suspects to betray themselves. Don't let your guard down by underestimating whom you're dealing with.

5. **I'm weak—help me**
   They act weak to get your sympathy, but don't be fooled. Think of Scarlett O'Hara! If you make concessions, be sure to get something in return. Don't drop your guard.

5

Tactics for Negotiating Abroad

Due to our relative prosperity in the 20th century, North Americans have fallen behind the rest of the world when it comes to negotiation. What we think of as bad manners, many cultures regard as normal bargaining. In some cultures, the failure to negotiate aggressively is taken as an insult.

> **What we think of as bad manners, many cultures regard as normal bargaining.**

When you negotiate abroad, consider the following:

1. **Show respect for other cultures.**
   The haughty attitude of many Americans is offensive to people whose cultures are much older than ours. Don't expect everyone to act like an American. If you are planning a business trip overseas, read up on the culture you will be visiting.

2. **Exercise patience.**
   Patience seems to be everybody else's strength and our weakness. Whether we're discussing the Pacific Rim, Latin America, or the Middle East, patience is a hallmark of negotiation behavior. Negotiations can be extremely slow-moving by our standards.

3. **Nurture personal relationships.**
   Personal relationships are often the basis of business relationships. Unlike our impersonal way of doing business, many cultures emphasize the blending of business and personal activities. In Japan, for example, it takes a long time to be accepted. Deals are sealed with personal guarantees rather than contracts. That probably accounts for the small number of lawyers in Japan (approximately 10,000).

4. **Be prepared to negotiate off the record.**
   Much of the serious transaction of business overseas occurs in informal sessions. In contrast to our conference room mentality, more business is conducted off the record.

Become aware of the many tactics you will encounter overseas. Be ready to identify each tactic you observe. Once you have unmasked the tactic, you can determine how you want to react.

Self-Check: Chapter 5 Review

Answers to these questions appear on page 97.

1. List three ways you can deal with negotiators who scream and yell at you.

   a. _____

   b. _____

   c. _____

2. If a customer tells you that he or she has a limited budget, what should you do?

   _____

   _____

3. What are two ways to deal with a nibble?

   a. _____

   b. _____

4. If new information is introduced during a negotiation, you should

   _____

5. What are two ways of dealing with an ultimatum?

   a. _____

   b. _____

Chapter *Six*

Strategies for Cooperative Negotiating

Chapter Objectives

▶ Follow three rules for win-win negotiating.

▶ Communicate effectively for a cooperative result.

W hen we think of negotiation as a contest, conflict occurs because we are more concerned with getting what we want than with attempting to understand each other's needs and emotions. We become defensive about our respective positions.

When both parties communicate their needs and feelings, the need to be defensive disappears. By understanding and accepting each other, we can transcend our individual positions and focus on solving the problem together. We switch from arguing over positions to collaborative problem solving.

Following Three Rules for Win-Win Negotiating

The ultimate goal of win-win negotiation is the creation of long-term, cooperative relationships. We have more to gain from working together than from growing apart. By following the Three Rules for Win/Win Negotiating, we can move beyond conflict to collaboration, as illustrated in the following diagram.

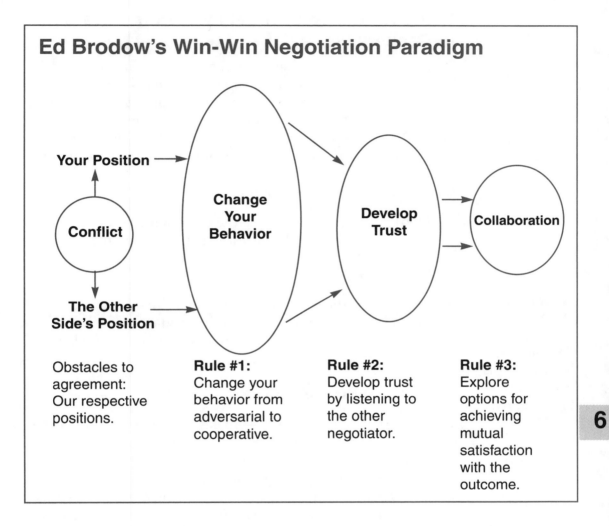

Ed Brodow's Win-Win Negotiation Paradigm

Your Position →

Conflict

The Other
Side's Position →

Change
Your
Behavior

Develop
Trust

Collaboration

Obstacles to
agreement:
Our respective
positions.

Rule #1:
Change your
behavior from
adversarial to
cooperative.

Rule #2:
Develop trust
by listening to
the other
negotiator.

Rule #3:
Explore
options for
achieving
mutual
satisfaction
with the
outcome.

6

Rule #1: Change Your Behavior from Adversarial to Cooperative

The way we behave is what encourages trust, cooperation, and agreement. The way you negotiate in itself may meet some of the other negotiator's needs. Satisfaction comes less from getting the result you want than from how you negotiate with each other. If other negotiators approach you with hostility, you can defuse their negative attitude and emotions by changing yours.

Overcome your negative emotions.

◆ Don't get trapped into using the other side's negative approach. If they are hostile, it may put you on the defensive. You may be inclined to mirror their hostility. This kind of reaction is counterproductive.

◆ Don't adopt the worst interpretation of their behavior. Instead of reacting to their hostility, find out what is motivating their behavior. They won't seem so bad when you understand them better.

Instead of reacting to their hostility, find out what is motivating their behavior.

Create a cooperative environment.

◆ Don't act like an adversary—make it easier for the other side to cooperate with you. If you approach them with a hostile attitude—that is, if you act like their adversary—they will respond in kind by being hostile to you. But if you behave in a cooperative manner—if you show them that you respect their interests—then they will respond by respecting yours. It's called *leading by example.*

◆ Don't try to win. Try to understand them. The objective is not to win, but to solve the problem inherent in the negotiation. In the baseball strike that lasted for eight months, we observed both sides attempting to win and failing to solve the problem. The problem was how to apportion the resources for mutual satisfaction.

◆ Show respect for other negotiators by treating them with dignity. Many employer-employee disputes could be resolved if the employer would show more respect for the employee's sense of dignity. Telling an employee, "I'm the boss, do what I say," creates animosity. The approach that says, "Let's share each other's concerns," produces motivated employees.

Show respect for other negotiators by treating them with dignity.

◆ Don't offend their egos. Remember that each of us wants to be perceived and treated in a certain way. If you offend someone's sense of self, you will create an adversary.

◆ If they continue to be hostile or uncooperative, let them know how their behavior will have a negative impact on solving the problem (as opposed to telling another person that he or she is being a jerk).

Share information.

◆ Define your positions on the issues.

◆ Where do you agree?

◆ Where do you disagree?

◆ How did the differences come about? The objective here is to create a better understanding of each other's point of view.

6

Put yourself in their shoes.

◆ When you see things from their point of view, it will be easier for you to accept their behavior and easier for you to find a way to help them be satisfied with the negotiation outcome.

Take a Moment

Select a recent negotiation. How could you have changed your behavior to encourage a cooperative atmosphere?

_____

_____

_____

_____

_____

_____

_____

Rule #2: Develop Trust by Listening to the Other Side's Concerns

Show that you care.

> **When you really listen to them, other negotiators will know that you care about them and their interests.**

◆ Listen. When you really listen to them, other negotiators will know that you care about them and their interests. Don't interrupt them. After they've had a chance to be heard, they will be more receptive to hearing you.

◆ Ask them about their interests.

◆ Ask them for the reason they are taking their positions.

◆ Get their help. Ask their advice in finding solutions.

◆ Let them think it was their idea!

◆ If they are upset, offer an apology.

◆ Look for opportunities to agree—find common ground instead of focusing on where you disagree.

Develop trust by demonstrating that you trust the other side.

◆ Confront the adversarial situation by communicating needs and feelings. In a cooperative negotiation, it is appropriate to share your problems and concerns with the other negotiator. While it may be wise to limit the outflow of such information in a negotiation with someone you don't know, it begins to make less sense when you want to create a long-term relationship with the other side.

> **Confront the adversarial situation by communicating needs and feelings.**

Acknowledge their position instead of arguing with them.

◆ Most people expect an argument. Saying, "Yes, I understand how you feel," can be very disarming. They may follow your lead and open up to you.

Express your position as an addition to theirs instead of as a disagreement.

◆ Let them know your interests may not be diametrically opposed to theirs. For example, suppose you are selling a product to a buyer who declares that your price is too high. Instead of telling them that they are wrong (that your price is standard for the industry), you can sympathize with their concern about rising prices and then explain how your company's costs have been rising.

Woo them. Show them that you want to work with them.

◆ It is very difficult to resist someone who appears genuinely interested in you and your interests.

List the interests both of you have in common.

◆ Once you establish common ground, it will be easier to resolve your differences.

Maintain open communication via frequent meetings.

◆ Trust is encouraged by keeping each other up to date.

6

Take a Moment

What steps could you have taken in a recent negotiation to develop a trusting atmosphere?

_____

_____

_____

_____

_____

Rule #3: Explore Options for Achieving Mutual Satisfaction with the Outcome

If the other side feels they are participating in the process, they will be more committed to the resolution. The operative word here is *collaboration*. In an adversarial negotiation, the two sides are working at opposite ends of a contest. In a cooperative negotiation, both sides work together in a collaborative enterprise. The objective is an agreement which satisfies—fulfills the needs of—both parties.

Disputes disappear when you collaborate on solving the problem.

Focus on the problem.

◆ Deadlocked negotiations are the result of focusing on individual positions. Get away from positions. Get away from personalities. Disputes disappear when you collaborate on solving the problem. Use the word "we." When you approach a negotiation in this way, you will notice the absence of the anxiety that accompanies an adversarial negotiation. The object is no longer for each side to get what it wants at the expense of the other. The object now is to work together to maximize mutual satisfaction.

Brainstorm the problem with them.

◆ It's amazing what you can come up with if you put your heads together. Be creative. Consider any and all possibilities. The negative energy of a contest is replaced by the synergistic energy of the collaboration.

> **Be creative. Consider any and all possibilities.**

Ask their preference among several options.

◆ Offer different potential approaches. Broaden the possibilities instead of focusing on only one solution.

  • Which way do you prefer?

  • What if we tried this?

Help them to save face.

◆ They need to look good to others. They also need to be able to justify the agreement to themselves. The concept of *face saving* means that they can justify doing something other than what they first had in mind.

  • Show how circumstances have changed since they came up with their old position.

  • Appeal to objective criteria/standards. Use the force of legitimacy.

  • Appeal to a third party (mediator). Many labor disputes are resolved in this manner.

  • Make a concession that they can show to whomever they need to impress.

6

Do research.

◆ What have others done in similar situations? This can help guide your search for mutual satisfaction.

Ask an expert for advice.

◆ Getting the input of an expert can clear up misunderstandings and introduce information that otherwise would not be available to either side.

Break the agreement up into parts.

| Establish agreement on as many things as possible. | ◆ Establish agreement on as many things as possible. After you both become aware of the issues on which you do agree, it will be easier to resolve the issues of contention. |

Expand the pie.

◆ Bring added value into the negotiation. I negotiated a better price on the design for my promotional brochures by offering consulting services to my graphic designer. Her unwillingness to budge on the price disappeared when we added a new value to the negotiation—she needed my advice on how to market her services at higher prices. We were able to agree on the price I wanted by adding in my consulting services as part of the deal. What other values can you add to your negotiation?

Take a Moment

What additional values could have been included in one of your most recent negotiations? How could you have expanded the pie?

_____

_____

_____

If you follow these Three Rules for Win-Win Negotiating, you will be able to convert your adversarial negotiations into cooperative ones. Now let's explore some of the ways in which we can communicate our ideas constructively.

Communicating Constructively

In this section, we will focus on two skills which are necessary if you are to become a first-class cooperative negotiator—listening and asking questions.

Next to the willingness to challenge everything, the most important skill for negotiators is listening. Nothing works better to create trust and cooperation than listening. The advantage of being a good listener is that the other negotiator will tell you everything you need to create a win-win outcome. Most people are not good listeners, yet listening is not a very difficult art to master. In fact, it's quite simple.

> **Next to the willingness to challenge everything, the most important skill for negotiators is listening.**

Actually, it's similar to what I go through in order to keep physically fit. The easy part of staying fit is doing all the exercises. That's right, the exercising is the easy part. The hard part is getting to the gym every day. The excuses I come up with for not going are amazing. Once I get to the health club, I'm home free.

6

Learning how to listen is the same. The hard part—the equivalent of "getting to the gym"—is being quiet. If you can train yourself to keep quiet most of the time, you will be a great listener . . . and a great negotiator.

Listening Like a Negotiator

Successful negotiators resemble the television detective Columbo—they ask questions and listen. Here is how you can emulate Columbo:

♦ **Develop the desire to listen.**
You must accept the fact that listening to others is your strongest weapon. Given the opportunity, the other negotiator will tell you everything you need to know. If this doesn't create desire, I don't know what will.

♦ **Always let the other person do most of the talking.**
This is a simple matter of mathematics. You talk 30 percent of the time, you allow them to talk 70 percent of the time.

Always let the other person do most of the talking.

♦ **Don't interrupt.**
There is always the temptation to interrupt so you can tell the other person something you think is vitally important. It isn't, so don't. When you are about to speak, ask yourself if it is really necessary.

♦ **Learn *active listening*.**
It's not enough that you're listening to someone—you want to be sure that they know you're listening. *Active listening* is the art of communicating to them that you're hearing their every word.

♦ **Always ask the other person to clarify what he or she just said.**
This will clear up any misunderstanding you have.

♦ **Learn to "listen" for nonverbal messages—body language.**
The other negotiator may be communicating with you via body language—you need to decode the message.

♦ **Ask a question . . . then be quiet.**
This is a foolproof way to listen. Think of yourself as an interviewer—you're Barbara Walters!

Tips for Asking Questions

Once you have learned how to keep yourself from speaking, the art of asking questions is the shortcut to effective listening.

◆ **Ask open-ended questions.**
Open-ended questions are questions that can't be answered with a simple yes or no. "How could we do this?" "What do you think?" Your objective is to get them to talk as much as possible.

◆ **Don't ask questions that put the other person on the defensive.**
For example, "Why?" is intimidating. Don't ask "why?" Ask "how come?"

◆ **Ask "What if?"**
What if we did it this way?

◆ **Ask for the other person's advice.**
"What would you suggest we do to resolve this?" Everyone loves to be asked for advice.

◆ **Offer alternatives.**
"Which way would you prefer?" This demonstrates your respect for the other negotiator.

◆ **Ask about the other person's feelings.**
"How do you feel about this, Ed?"

◆ **Repeat back what the other person said.**
"Let me be sure I understand what you're saying. You're saying that . . . ?" This technique will prevent misunderstandings and convince them that you really are listening.

The material in Chapter 6 can change not only the way you negotiate in business but also the way you approach each of the relationships in your life. This represents a major paradigm shift. Instead of regarding other people as "the enemy," view them as potential partners. Instead of reacting defensively to differences of opinion, focus on the problem to be solved and the opportunity for mutual satisfaction. Begin right away!

6

The art of asking questions is the shortcut to effective listening.

Self-Check: Chapter 6 Review

Answers to these questions appear on page 97.

1. The essence of win-win negotiating is switching from an argument over your respective positions to

   _____

   _____

2. The first thing you must do to create a win-win situation is

   _____

   _____

3. The most effective way to gain people's trust is to

   _____

4. List four ways you can help other negotiators to save face.

   a. _____

   b. _____

   c. _____

   d. _____

5. In order to listen effectively, you should talk _____ percent of the time and allow others to talk _____ percent of the time.

6. Focus on an upcoming negotiation. How can you apply the Three Rules for Win-Win Negotiating?

_____

_____

_____

_____

_____

_____

_____

6

Chapter *Seven*

Making Negotiation Work for You

Chapter Objectives

▶ Review the steps you must follow in a negotiation.

▶ Create your own personal Negotiation Action Plan.

▶ Launch yourself on your personal homework assignment.

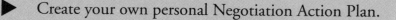

L et's review three basic steps in your path toward a successful negotiation.

Three Steps for a Successful Negotiation

1. Prepare for Every Negotiation

Thinking of yourself as a detective, you must gather pertinent information about the other negotiator. How do they view the negotiation? What is their motivation? At the same time, you need to be aware of your own motivation. What will satisfy you?

Next, you must decide upon the optimum number of negotiators. Is this a solo operation, or does this situation justify a team? Where do you want to conduct the negotiation? What should be in the agenda?

2. Develop Your Strategy

Creating a strategy will require an evaluation of your relationship with the other negotiator. If trust has been established from an existing relationship, you can proceed with a win-win strategy to explore options for mutual satisfaction. Allow the trust to carry you over the goal line.

If you are beginning a new relationship, you need to focus your behavior into cooperative channels. Aim to create a cooperative atmosphere where trust can be developed.

If, on the other hand, you are dealing with an adversarial negotiator, you can develop a strategy from your arsenal of competitive techniques.

3. Implement Your Strategy

Remember that negotiation is the process of overcoming obstacles to reach agreement. What are the obstacles to reaching your agreement?

> **Remember that negotiation is the process of overcoming obstacles to reach agreement.**

- ◆ If the obstacles center around issues, establish the issues where you already have agreement and then move to the areas of contention. Develop trust by listening to the other side's point of view. Woo them. Let them know that you understand their interests and want to help them to achieve satisfaction. Then brainstorm the problem areas until you uncover a workable solution.

- ◆ If the obstacles are the people, change your behavior from adversarial to cooperative. Don't respond to hostility with hostility. Put yourself in their shoes. Your effort to understand the other negotiator's position and needs will enable you to avoid personality-based disputes. Remember to focus on solving the problem. When they see that you are cooperative rather than hostile, they will follow your example.

- ◆ If the obstacle is that you are dealing with an adversarial negotiator, then you can defend yourself. Open with an extreme position. Lower their expectations. Keep your mouth shut. Don't be afraid to walk away. At the same time, you can break down the walls using the Three Rules for Win-Win Negotiating.

7

Your Negotiation Action Plan

Here is a simplified step-by-step process for you to follow in your next negotiation. You may want to keep a copy of this handy.

- ◆ Have I established my targets?
  - Maximum?
  - Goal?
  - Bottom Line?

- ◆ Do I understand my real interests—what do I really need to achieve in this negotiation?

- ◆ Where should I start?

- ◆ What concessions am I willing to make?

- ◆ What are my options?

- ◆ What are my strengths?

- ◆ What is the pressure on the other side?

- ◆ What are their real needs?

- ◆ What are their options?

- ◆ What are the deadlines in this negotiation? Are they negotiable?

- Are there any mutually acceptable standards/objective criteria we can use to reach agreement?

- What should be in the agenda?

- Where should we hold the negotiation?

- How many negotiators should we have?

- How can I help the other side feel satisfied?

- Do we have a trusting relationship?

- What can I do to create a cooperative environment?

- Am I concentrating on being a good listener?

- Have I identified the common ground in the negotiation—where do we agree?

- What interests do we have in common?

- What options exist for mutual satisfaction?

- How can we expand the pie?

7

Try It: Your Personal Homework Assignment

Take advantage of the many opportunities in your life for negotiation.

To help yourself develop negotiation consciousness, you need to practice—by taking advantage of the many opportunities in your life for negotiation. Instead of passing up these opportunities, approach them with a sense of fun. It isn't necessary that you win, but it is important to practice being assertive.

◆ Negotiate at the supermarket.

◆ Negotiate with your credit card company for better interest rates or for waiver of the annual fee.

◆ Negotiate at the gas station.

◆ Negotiate for a free upgrade on your next commercial flight.

◆ Negotiate for a better deal on your new car, television set, refrigerator, furniture, clothing, audio equipment, computer, etc.

◆ Begin to question what you read in the newspapers and hear on television—develop your critical faculties.

It's like the old one-liner, "Excuse me, how do I get to Carnegie Hall?" The answer, "Practice!"

In Closing

Most people in our culture have been taught that negotiation is more to be feared than enjoyed. As a result of reading this book:

1. You now understand more about the negotiation process than 99 percent of your peers.

2. You have the resources to integrate the negotiation process into your life so that you will look forward to each new opportunity to negotiate.

3. Your understanding of how to create a cooperative atmosphere can change your life.

Realistically, you will encounter some situations that do not conform to the win-win paradigm. That is why we have devoted time to competitive techniques. But I hope you always will make the effort to implement the win-win approach. When it comes to negotiation, a collaboration is much more productive than a contest. Either way you now possess the tools to negotiate with confidence.

You now understand more about the negotiation process than 99 percent of your peers.

7

Answers to Selected Exercises

Chapter 1

Take a Moment, page 14

1. Your position: You won't pay more than $16,000.

2. Your real interest: You want to impress your neighbor by not paying more than she did for the car—$18,000. (*Ego* and *acceptance of others*)

3. The dealer's position: He won't sell the car for less than $20,000.

4. The dealer's real interest: He wants to receive the incentive bonus from the manufacturer before the month is up. (*Material gain* and *time*)

5. The interests of both sides can be accommodated by making a deal at $18,000. You get to match your neighbor's price, and the dealer qualifies for his bonus.

Chapter Review, page 15

1. Negotiation is the process of <u>overcoming obstacles</u> to <u>reach agreement.</u>

2. A good deal in negotiation is one in which <u>satisfaction</u> is achieved.

3. a. Adversarial
   b. Cooperative (Win-Win)

4. Our basic interests in a negotiation have to do with our <u>motivation.</u>

5. Many of us have a negative attitude toward negotiation because we perceive it as a <u>contest.</u> We can overcome this negativity by perceiving negotiation as a <u>collaboration.</u>

Chapter 3

Chapter Review, page 45

1. Goal: The result we'll be satisfied to achieve.

2. Bottom line: The worst outcome we will accept under pressure in order to make a deal.

3. a. Information about yourself.
   b. Information about the other side.
   c. Information about industry standards and objective criteria.
   d. Information about the agenda.

4. Choose from:
   a. Having options
   b. Remaining patient
   c. Possessing information
   d. Demonstrating commitment
   e. Showing persistence
   f. Taking risks
   g. Having legitimacy
   h. Showing weakness

5. Answers will vary.

6. Answers will vary.

Chapter 4

Take a Moment, page 50

Answers could include:
1. Informing the dealer that your present car doesn't run anymore.
2. Admitting that you love the dealer's car so much, you won't buy anything else.
3. Letting the dealer know that the competition doesn't have this car in stock.
4. Allowing your spouse to tell the dealer, "I just love this model!"

Take a Moment, page 51

Answers could include:

1. Telling the dealer that you're not in any hurry to buy a car.
2. Complaining about how the car performs or how it looks.
3. Letting the dealer know about competition from other dealerships or other makes.
4. Having your spouse say, "I liked the car we saw yesterday much better."

Chapter Review, page 61

1. Choose from:
   a. Give them a meaningful explanation.
   b. Give them a minor concession.
   c. Stroke their egos.
   d. Give them an ultimatum.
   e. Listen to them.

2. In an adversarial negotiation, you will raise the other side's expectations if you <u>disclose information that is damaging to your position.</u>

3. Large concessions convey a message of <u>weakness.</u>

4. Whenever you give something away, you should <u>get something in return.</u>

5. a. It may force the other side to compromise.
   b. It provides the other negotiators with ammunition to convince their boss to make the deal on your terms.
   c. It demonstrates your commitment to your position.

Chapter 5

Chapter Review, page 73

1. a. Allow them to vent their feelings.
   b. Empathize with them without agreeing to anything.
   c. When they calm down, ask them what they really want.

2. Recognize what she or he is doing and maintain your expectations.

3. Choose from:
   a. Show them a price list.
   b. Claim limited authority to make concessions.
   c. Pretend it's a joke and say, "No."
   d. Include the nibbled item in your price.
   e. Hold them to their agreement.

4. Insist on adequate time to prepare for the new situation.

5. a. Challenge it.
   b. Ignore it.

Chapter 6

Chapter Review, page 86

1. The essence of win-win negotiating is switching from an argument over your respective positions to collaborative problem solving.

2. The first thing you must do to create a win-win situation is to change your behavior from adversarial to cooperative.

3. The most effective way to gain people's trust is to listen to them.

4. a. Show how circumstances have changed since they came up with their old position.
   b. Appeal to objective criteria/standards.
   c. Appeal to a third party (mediator).
   d. Make a concession that they can show to whomever they need to impress.

5. In order to listen effectively, you should talk underline{30} percent of the time and allow others to talk underline{70} percent of the time.

6. Answers will vary.